Painting In
The Dark

Cover Design: TreManda Pewett

Editor: Carla Dupont Huger & Sarah Plamondon

Illustration: TreManda Pewett

ISBN-13: 978-0-9862556-6-3
ISBN-10: 0-9862556-6-1

Jeanius Publishing LLC

430 Lee Blvd

Lehigh Acres, FL 33936

For more information, please visit:

Jeaniuspublishing.com

Painting In The Dark

by KJWhite

Jeanius
PUBLISHING

I am not an author or a poet,
I am an artist
making my best effort to paint
with colors that can be heard and
sounds that can be seen
even in the darkest of rooms.

So thank you for listening to
the strokes of my paintbrush.
Enjoy!

I appreciate you!

If the ground was the sky

would you still want to fly?

-contentment

She made love twice,

and made love four times

-*my best friends*

How magical is color?

The awe of a rainbow,
or paint on a canvas that whisper
stories of unspoken feelings.
Lies with subtle truths,
where words like *almost*
become the fingerprint of honesty;
almost red or *almost* blue,
maybe teal or scarlet.
"What do you think?"
....
....
....
(tosses me a football)

-Athletics > expression

How about I die
and go to the mortuary
so they can
remove all of my organs and
make space for your hand.
I'm sure I can live up
to your dreams then.

My bones have been broken
by words countless times;
words that imprisoned me
behind the bars of my Hershey skin.
Words with teeth that ate at my soul
and melted my self-esteem,
like fallen chocolate on a summer playground.
They would eat me alive and I would just smile
but in my soul,
I felt every tooth ripping into my confidence
I felt every bite

- *4th grade*

My grandmother used to ask me to throw out her cigarettes,

putting cancer in my fingers as if I didn't want to taste death myself.

I always replied with, "Yes ma'am," and walked around her house

longing to be alone so I could go for the kill. How ironic

smoke clouded the rooms of her home when I visited

and I couldn't wait to smother my lungs with the glorious squares,

Grandma always called them squares,

but I never knew why until I became an adult

my grandmother was a prophet

foreseeing the box that it would lead her to

and accepting the karma beforehand

I just pray my words fell deaf to death's ears,

when I was around grandma's house ,

with grandma's squares

I watched my parents fight like cats and dogs,

then get along like cats and dogs,

they even loved us like cats and dogs,

one minute they're full of kisses and overprotective,

the next, you don't see them for days.

I've seen my mother wear sunlight and darkness in the same hour;

at 3:52 she laughed so hard

the entire car shook,

I just stared at her, and absorbed her warmth;

I loved the summer.

at 3:53 she faced me

to ask what I'd like to eat,

her left eye was black and swollen

and I just stared at her,

because I was still afraid of the dark.

"I hate you!"

"who cares.....my kids don't"

"those aren't your kids..."

"......what?"

- the day she hit him back

I'm not upset at you for not being there.

I'm upset at you for not being there enough.

I wanted more than a few dollars here and there

and stories about life before me,

as if you wished for a time machine

to go back to the good ol' days before I was your burden.

I wanted you at my games and award ceremonies

to embarrass me with, "That's my boy!" after proud moments.

I wanted advice about girls

and what to do about the butterflies in my stomach.

I wanted your attention

you may have been around

but you certainly weren't present.

- Happy Father's Day

You call it trauma,

I call it tomorrow

-is this normal?

I'm glad that I smile like you

and have your prominent features.

I'm glad that you gave me "the talk" when I was 11.

I'm sorry for pulling away from you

when all you wanted was a hug from me

after a long day.

I wanted you to be the perfect mother to me

when perfect was nowhere in your name.

My friends adored you and I couldn't see it

until we became friends and

I fell in love with the person you truly are.

you weren't perfect, but you were mine

that's more than enough

- mama

I don't wish

that I could have had flawless parents.

I just wish my parents would have explored

the gifts they birthed in me.

Now, they will only know

where that journey could have taken them

when my life unwraps to become the gift

they were originally designed to become

My brother

went to the gym

went home to relax

passed out in the hallway

went to the emergency room

went into surgery

and

went into Heaven

what just happened....

KJWhite

I'm still wondering how

a licensed

professional

doctorate holding

surgeon

expects **ANYONE** to survive

with no oxygen to their brain

during hours of heart surgery.

I guess they thought he was a superhero too

or

still needed hours to walk across the stage.

- I hope you graduated with honors

I accepted that you're gone

and I know you're in a better place

but

if it's ok with you

please

don't go

Words bounced off your casket

like the rain as you dropped into the earth;

I guess you're bullet proof to pain now.

So I know you can't hear me,

because every word

carries a tear of its own.

- please stay...

We went through so much together,

from making forts out of furniture,

to beds out of backseats and homes out of hotels;

life was never ideal for us.

But even when we didn't have a solid meal,

we always had each other to fill our stomachs

with cramps from laughter until we passed out

on the living room floor.

Our dedication to keep one another

raised us to the men we've come to know

promising each other to never become what caused us

so much lack growing up

And 'til this day, we have kept that promise.

I couldn't have asked for better siblings,

which is why I questioned God

when the doctor said, "that one took a turn for the worse."

You fought like crazy to be with us forever,

but after 21 years of giving all you had,

you were called to dine with the angels.

I saw a part of our mother leave when you did.

I saw my father cry for the first time.

Even the clouds mourned your loss with hours of rainfall.

But as the sun appeared again,

I found peace in knowing you no longer had to fight.

I still hurt from your loss.

To know that there were once 4 of us,

and then there were 3.

And it will always be that way until we

reunite on the streets of gold.

I am now older than you ever got a chance to reach.

But you will always be my big brother.

- 1984-2005

KJWhite

I sat down at my table,

gave my heart a pen and told it to write.

As ink spilled on the pages,

so did all the things I never said.

She says all men are the same; that we only want one thing
and that I'm different without the offer to prove myself.
There are so many empty words in our conversations
where I'm left wondering,
what she really thinks of me;
like a brother I'm sure.

I am tissue for her runny nose,
the glue to her fragile mindset
when she is used over and over again,
as nothing more than a text at 2 a.m.

What do I see in you...

there was

always something

about you.

this thing

that I knew I never needed

but always craved.

this

sweet poison

you offered.

- I'm dying to taste it

KJWhite

sometimes

getting what you wished for

makes you wish

you never seen

a shooting

star

we experimented

with our interpretation of love

mixing flavors that were never meant for one another

like an ocean on the sun

trying to find paradise in the depths of its lust.

we experimented

but couldn't create the solution to fix

what was never there.

- *chemistry*

me tapping out of our arguments

does not mean that

you are correct.

It just means that

I am tired of wrestling your mind,

to be accepting of my opinions.

I became friends with your body

but have yet to meet your mind;

and no matter how good it feels to be near to you,

it's clear, that we are better when we are apart.

Though truth has separated us many times,

our lips always connected us again

finding ways to speak without poetry,

ways without expression.

why talk it out,

when we can just kiss?

- problem solved

We went to church in each other's arms Saturday nights,

and fell asleep

when we went church Sunday morning.

Our bodies were

playgrounds of worship;

false religions that carried no power

other than the magic of making up,

which was nothing more

than smoke and mirrors.

what do you mean when you tell me to, "be a man?"
am I not a man because I love recklessly and
aren't ashamed to say that I cry sometimes?
am I not a man for admitting that I have a confidence dilemma
for being truthful enough to say that rejection
has fractured my hope time and time again?

I confess, I am strong; but I am also weak.
the broadness of my muscular chest and shoulders play no role
in carrying the burden of a broken heart
like you, I recover with time.
I cannot meet the expectations of your 11th commandment,
"thou shalt not feel."
if that's what it takes to reach the heavens of your acceptance
I'll gladly rot in hell.

The true colors of a person

change with the eyes that view them.

Just ask the butterfly

observing the rainbow.

- ultraviolet

KJWhite

Day 1

I'd take a bullet for you

Day 100

I'd take you somewhere

drop you off

and leave

- you've changed

her mind was a road of stagnant dreams,

a journey down the same street time and time again.

she grabbed my hand and asked me to lead her,

while pulling me along to follow the nightmare

she called a relationship.

I did not want to be hers

let alone her leader,

so I settled as her shadow instead.

we are drowning in doubt and have become

paralyzed by our inability to say what we feel;

allowing beliefs based on what we have assumed

to paint pictures of a mystery love life we've never known;

rather than using truth as the life jacket to save us

from a sinking relationship

I've never been able to swim in words,
they're so much heavier than water

- some things are better left unsaid

I thought you were happy,

I thought we were getting married,

I thought you would have my first child.

You thought we needed work,

You thought I didn't care,

You thought I never loved you.

I couldn't hear your thoughts,

until you thought

we'd be best apart.

let's burn the ashes,

and start from the moment when

we really knew each other.

the moment when you

removed the makeup from your personality

and the moment I looked into your eyes

 and said, "I don't love you."

let's stop becoming pregnant with false expectations,

giving birth to disappointments and let downs.

let's start from the end of our story

let's start

from just not caring anymore.

The moment you walk in the door,

I patiently wait for you to leave.

but as soon as you're not around,

I can't wait

to see you again.

- when it doesn't make sense anymore

You were away a few days,
but every second
that passed without you,
felt like an eternity.

I longed for everything about you
I missed your smell, soft lips,
the way you aggravated me for no reason at all;
we met at your place, and I asked you
"How was your weekend?"

but what I heard come out of my mouth was,

"you cheated on me didn't you?"

silence crept in our lungs

as air departed from the room

and slowly,

your eyes began to rain.

I'd never felt hurt like this before,

I'd never felt so betrayed.

43

KJWhite

I didn't realize the pain you caused

until I awoke from the lying affections

I once knew as love.

My emotions

had taken my brain for granted

and left me naive to the obvious;

that we were destined for destruction

the moment we dared to build

with 2 broken people.

I was the skeleton in your treasure chest of rusted metal,

hidden from sight until you needed me to save the day.

I was your bird,

I was your plane,

I was your superman,

And you were my kryptonite

You saw me falling for you

you held out your arms to protect my feelings

you caught me

and robbed me of learning

not to love someone like you again

KJWhite

I'm amazed at how such harsh words

came from such delicate lips.

It's like kissing a dandelion

whose petals are made of needles and thorns.

refusing to acknowledge what is hidden in plain sight

is a suicide note

exclaiming that

you no longer want to breathe

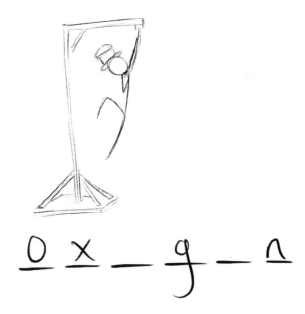

0 x _ g _ ∩

Had we studied one another,

we would never think to cheat

during the tests of our relationship.

We skip on the opportunities to spend time

with one another, as if it's an Algebra course

during final exams;

but our absences were unexcused

and we became truants of love.

By the time I was ready to learn of you

you

had already dropped out on me

I made a commitment to save myself until marriage;

then I married you

without ever putting a ring on your finger.

I didn't save anything,

but quarters to wash my bed sheets.

I grew weary in chasing what couldn't be caught;

wind between my fingers trying constantly to bottle the air in my palms.

she only wants to see me during vacations from him,

lay under my arms and cover herself in my shadows

wishing her reality wasn't so much work,

telling me I was the oxygen to her very existence

and I believed her.

But I guess my love was only convenient in seasons.

I made love to you,

while you had sex with me;

even told your friends our business

and asked if I was interested

in sharing parts of me

that I thought only you wanted to explore.

you see,

men aren't the only ones

who are dogs

I will not say that I hate you

because hate is a word of great strength

so I

strongly

                                                   forcibly

                           actively

vigorously

                                      substantially

tenaciously

                       aggressively

                                      fervently

dislike you.

I do not want to be the name that rolls off your tongue

when you are in ecstasy.

I will not be your comfort,

when you choose to lay your head on pillows of broken glass.

I am not your altered reality and

cannot make you feel the way "he did"

because I am not him, nor do I wish to be.

He may have made you feel like a woman,

but he will never

make you feel like a wife.

I find it amazing

how you pick up every call,

now that I don't want to talk to you.

- *I just want my things*

I supplied your demands

but couldn't raise your interest in us,

your lie ability was your only asset

so, my investment was in vain,

not everything appreciates with time

- bad stock

her idea of chivalry,

was for me to politely open my wallet.

my dreams were once my secret place,

my getaway from you

until you,

appeared there also.

reminding me that you were under my skin

that I'd given you the world

and you'd taken mine away.

that you were on my tongue

though I hated the very resemblance of your name;

everything looks and sounds like you,

like pain. like deceit. you are a harsh reality

that I can no longer escape in the nightmares

my dreams have become.

vague memories of her had furnished my being,

completely consuming

the walls of my consciousness;

I had no rest,

no peace in the hallways of my spirit.

only pictures of us.

mirrors began to question my identity

my shadow has begun to fade,

as I have become

the subject of transparency.

wanting to be open to new love,

but it sees straight through me.

there is nothing worse

than missing someone

that you shouldn't have found

in the first place

it's not really you that I miss,

it's the parts of my heart

that followed you out

- still bleeding

sometimes

it hurts to hold on just as much as it does to let go.

you just can't see the bleeding

until you open your hand.

I can't be mad at you anymore.

I've held hate hostage without a price for its ransom long enough,

and failed to acknowledge that you too

are only human,

a soul trapped in a fallen society

where mistakes are the closest we come to perfection.

I have been you.

I have lied and manipulated hearts into

selling themselves short in the long run.

I have caused the divorce between self and confidence,

exchanging my deceit for her purity

and my purity for the shadow of darkness.

I am not justifying your wrongs

are you guilty?

yes. you are.

but so am I. and I forgave myself

therefore, I forgive you as well.

KJWhite

Love should audition for you

and earn a spot in your heart.

Because it's those we give a stage

That will only act the part.

KJWhite

she is innocent

and wants nothing more than to be the antidote

to my misery. but there is no quick fix to depression.

she is a stitch to my punctures,

peroxide to my wounds,

but only a band aid to my insecurities.

- *i didn't mean to use you*

when I look into her eyes

I see the same pain that once had me captive;

the kind of hurt that imprisons the soul of the muse

and the heart of the poet.

She is often misunderstood and misinterpreted,

trading her love for lust

only to be left behind to fall for the thought

of falling for someone.

KJWhite

I am

ripping the beauty away from her fragile limbs

and tearing her to a single stem piece by piece;

throwing the remains to the grass where they

mourn the loss of what was once beautiful.

she is a flower

or at least she used to be.

-she loves me

-she loves me not

I played hide and seek with your feelings,

thinking you'd appreciate the chase

as we flirted with misery and curiosity;

hiding our true intentions and playing with

shovels of immaturity

seeing who could dig the deepest,

who could find the truth in the words we wouldn't say.

the fire begin to dim as our storms progressed
and the downpour of confusion flooded in;
cute nothings no longer intrigued her
she wanted more or nothing at all
but i...

only wanted to remain and wasn't ready to

caption our friendship.

she enjoyed my company

and I enjoyed being her guest;

the man who loved to visit and make her smile,

and the man who loved to disappear

to escape my fear of sincere commitment.

she's crowned me king to a place in her soul that only she knows.

a place where her deepest fears,

desires and insecurities have lived forever.

no one has been there, but there, we reign together

shoulder to shoulder, side by side

I have the key to her gates, while she resides on the outside of

mine.

she charms my mind and fascinates my being,

so I allow her to explore my heart

only to end at roads of nothingness where I meet her at the gate,

kiss her through my fence of insecurity,

and tell her she can't go any further.

she doesn't understand me

so, she asked "do you love me?"

I replied, I do

"do you trust me?" I said, I do

"will you let me in?" I said, I can't

When she asked me why,

I told her I was afraid of being hurt again.

she said I was selfish...

I didn't respond.

It's not love until you've seen the worst it has to offer

and still commit to making sacrifices that reach for the uncertainty,

grasping ahold of the realization that you will

lose sleep,

lose tears, and

lose pride,

but rather

take a chance at an eternity of togetherness

than go a lifetime shadowed by what could have been

- are you sure you love me?

"so ...what are we?"

"whatever you want us to be"

"...that's not a good answer"

"...i'm so sorry"

- *after we made love*

to be broken is the spark of being driven,

even if that drive is geared in the wrong direction.

Often, I am closed because I've been broken as well,

so forgive me,

I'm not frustrated at you when I'm giving you a piece of my mind,

I'm just mad at myself for being broken still

and not being able to give you the whole thing.

she told me she knew I didn't care;

that the language of my heart never

matched the verbiage of my tongue

that my words were a pretty envelope

stamped with emptiness

enclosed with falsehoods

and sealed with doubt

I could never deliver what I thought I felt

because even she didn't believe me

when I would whisper "I love you"

and proceed to undress her

sometimes the words that are supposed to build us up,

are the very words that build the walls

you deserve to be loved

but I do not deserve to love you.

- let me go

the silence has become louder than rooms of crying infants.

I can't bear the noise of nothingness any longer. in peace,

yet fighting to hear my imagination speak to tell me;

that I made the right decision,

that I'm still a good guy

that I haven't become a monster.

tell me that the noise is temporary.

deafen me to the truth

that alarms the ears of my mind.

KJWhite

I am the breath that you will never exhale,

the power to ignite your flames of passion

or blow them to dust to be swept away and disregarded,

A wind of confusion who's direction cannot be interpreted

I am always a mystery that remains to be seen.

so do yourself a favor

please,

don't follow me anymore,

I don't want to keep hurting you.

xoxo

- your heart

the hatred will paralyze you

from fresh love

if you want to feel again

you must

let go.

you have to.

KJWhite

sometimes

the 1 you passed up was the

sweetest thing next to honey dripping

from the trees of heaven.

so don't be surprised when the lips of your 10

taste like nothing but regret.

I want to apologize to you for not always being understanding

and showing your body more attention

than the details of your conversation.

I ask that you forgive me. I was taught to love with my body

and only to use my brain to get to yours;

A woman's name was a trophy, and

having it on my list of conquered queens was my validation as a
man

I guess that's why they call it game,

a game that I'm long retired from

and though it's too late, I want you to know that

I'm sorry.

Don't embrace the pain

longer than it wants to hurt you

its only when you let go

that the healing process can begin its journey

KJWhite

waiting for the 1 is not an easy journey

especially when numbers come in infinite amount

every gift comes with a purpose

yearning alongside a desire to become someone's everything

and every purpose comes with a gift

endowed with a readiness to bring everything to pass

and she

will be both to me

I can't wait to meet you,

fragmented stages on a set of bliss.

A familiar face in the memories of my deepest desires;

unmatched,

unknown.

I can't wait to meet you,

hold you,

play with your hair,

you. my other half. the love of my life,

I will wait for you.

you are a gift from God himself

clothed in the tenderness of heaven and a smile that

leads the blind to see

like a waterfall over a bed of diamonds

hidden afar to be found as lost riches

there is no map to your heart

no secrets to your substance

She's even more stunning
to think about than to see in person
more beautiful to ponder upon
than to explore

KJWhite

her voice

is spring water

my ears are a deep well

waiting to be filled with her every thought

- I could listen to her talk for hours

My heart stopped the first time my eyes connected with hers,

in that moment I knew

that I longed for love more than life itself

to breathe through her kisses

as we slow danced with our tongues

to hold her so closely that

we'd become a synchronized heartbeat;

a harmonized soul

- the moment we meet

KJWhite

She was not my first kiss
but she was the first woman
to put poetry on my tongue

"so...what do you think of me?"

"all the time"

- *love has a mind of its own*

your body is begging to be held again

to fall into arms that would wrap around you like

belts made of open palms

to be moved by thundering whispers

and captivated as the sun diving under deep waters

you bring out the best in me

>the atmosphere of spring to my winter thoughts,

reminding me that the grass is never greener on the other side

>when we nurture our fields of uncertainty;

you assure me

>that I don't have to be an emblem of perfection

>for you to wear my name as a badge of honor,

>proud to call me your man

>and dying to call me your husband

I am appreciative of you

>and though you think

>men don't think about these things

>we do.

She is

a rose on a desert plain blooming against all odds

having been stepped on and over countless times

but rising so gracefully until her beauty

is brought to perfection

she is more than her pedals

she is

a fighter

she does not want to be independent

but would rather be alone

than with a man who measures her worth

by the curves that dress her frame

yes

she is a work of art

but you cannot buy her

she is not for sale

do not break her into pieces

and call her crazy when she starts to fall apart;

too often men have played doctor with empty promises in her
ears,

vowing their motives as a surgery

to put her together again;

only to end with a failed attempt from a sad excuse of a man.

blaming her for following through with the operation

knowing he never graduated

from the school of mended hearts

I cannot promise you forever

But I can promise

to make every moment we're together

feel like an eternity

she is music to my soul

the dazzling keys of an unblemished piano

that I so desperately want to play

a marvelous symphony

a beautiful composition

she is a breath of fresh air to a man who'd only known suffocation

You're beautiful to me, not because you're beautiful to me,

But because you're an open book;

An open book of brokenness, shattered and never rebuilt like the Tower of Babel,

Yet held together so extravagantly, that one would never know you've been hurt before,

Your emotions, played with, like an open surgery on a playground of thieves,

Left empty, feeling the pulse of your heart beat in another's hand,

Only to be left in abandonment, alone, shipwrecked

In a vast ocean, to be hooked again by the worm of deceit.

You're beautiful to me, not because you're beautiful to me,

But because you love hard, so hard its painful;

Needles and thorns on the foot of a slave chasing freedom,

Reaching for the light with lashes on her back,

Found and drug back to the fields to increase the body of art with chains and whips,

Like 15 hours of labor only to find no breath in the child you've housed for 9 months.

your scars

are not tombstones for the past experiences to haunt you,

but celebrations of the strength that clothe your courage,

reminders

that even when the damage is the deepest

even when it hurts more than ever,

it still could not break you

you are not a walking graveyard,

you are poetry with a beating heart

and your scars are your trophies

you are a champion

waking up to you will be a blessing that I am unworthy of receiving

a man who has hurt so many given the chance to

nurture such a beautiful mind.

I consider myself lucky to await this moment

to catch every tear and embrace you for the woman life has made you

to be, everything you deserve and beyond

you are amazing; you are breathtaking

and most importantly

you are mine

thank you,

for trusting me with your heart

Love,

your future husband

The End

Made in the USA
Middletown, DE
26 December 2017